QUIET THOUGHTS

SUDIE J. BRADLEY

WESTBOW
PRESS®
A DIVISION OF THOMAS NELSON
& ZONDERVAN

WestBow Press books may be ordered through booksellers or by contacting:

WestBow Press
A Division of Thomas Nelson & Zondervan
1663 Liberty Drive
Bloomington, IN 47403
www.westbowpress.com
844-714-3454

ISBN: 978-1-6642-3984-5 (sc)
ISBN: 978-1-6642-3985-2 (e)

Library of Congress Control Number: 2021913685

Print information available on the last page.

WestBow Press rev. date: 07/23/2021

CONTENTS

A Thought... 1

Why?... 2

Service Done 5

The Test 6

Give and Receive.. 7

Little One 8

The Voice of God 11

Faith 12

Peace Be Still...15

Endure 16

Serve 17

Love Is 19

Act 2 20

When One Questions 21

The Grand Lady.. 22

You Are Special 23

My Father's House 24

Thoughts.. 25

My Prayer... 27

Teaching: No Greater Call 28

On Being Black... 29

Jesus the Christ 30

The Holy Ghost.. 31

Adversity 32

Great and Terrible Days 35

You Are Beautiful.. 36

Service.. 37

Slow of Tongue 38

That Tiny Sin 39

I Cry 40

Death.. 41

Today's Precious Woman.. 42

Find the Blessing.. 45

Listen 46

Come unto Me.. 47

Pain—Joy... 48

Special Truths 49

Most Precious Gift 50

Take My Hand...51

Strength in Unity 52

The Living Angel.. 53

My Testimony... 54

Today's Pioneers 55

Communication 56

Teenager: Half Child, Half Grown........................... 57

Come 58

Spiritual Levels.. 59

The Phone Call... 60

Joy in the Morning... 63

I Wonder.. 64

A Purpose... 65

A THOUGHT

As quietly as
> the morning dew,
> the falling snow,
> the warming rays.

As quietly as
> the growing grass,
> a flowering bud,
> a baby's laugh.

As quietly as these
> does a thought grow.

WHY?

A tiny seed within my heart
    Was planted there by One unseen.
It was so very long ago
    I almost forgot.

But then I heard a tiny voice
    Cry out from where the seed was imparted.
It spoke of love, of truth, and family,
    of honesty and respect.
It spoke not of color, but of light.
    Not of war, but of peace and right.
It guided me through trying plights.
    It asked only that I take its advice.

That tiny voice from deep within
    Cried out for more, more nourishment.
"What kind?" asked I, "and where?"
    "Fear not," that tiny voice cried out.
"For you will know and have no doubts."

SERVICE DONE

As the glow of a candle which pierces the night
　　With warmth and love and light,
The love of the Lord from deep within
　　Shines with a light so bright.
It welled itself up and shone all around
　　As service so aptly performed.
It tells of your love, your dedication
　　To serve as Christ would serve.

THE TEST

Each test that Thou giveth me
Seems just a little harder, a little more deep.
It seems designed to test my faith,
The strength of which I now hold in doubt.

And Thy Spirit, must it be withdrawn for the test?
Must I stand this trial alone?
Do not remove Thyself so far from me
For I fear I cannot stand alone.

My faith held strong; the test is won.
Thy Spirit flows in me.
Had not I stood that trial alone,
My faith, my love, would never have grown this strong.

GIVE AND RECEIVE

To be able to give
    is a wonderful thing.
It fills the heart of the giver
    with a sweetness unsurpassed.

To be able to receive
    is a greater task indeed.
It requires humbleness and much understanding
    which enlarges the heart.

To give and receive
    we need to taste of both.
One without the other
    is to grow but half the growth.

LITTLE ONE

Oh, little one, how my heart cries out as I watch you in the night.

A silent prayer comes tumbling, tumbling into my mind.

How I want to shield you from hurt and harm, from all life's negatives.

But alas, I know this will only cause thee harm.

You must learn to choose, to taste of hurt and sorrow, to know of joy and happiness.

Choose wisely, little one, for I will try, I will try to teach you the way.

I will guide you as those first steps you take to your Father, whose arms are outstretched to thee.

Oh, little one, how my heart cries out as I watch thee.

THE VOICE OF GOD

There is a calmness, an inner spring of hope
    that swells up, that fills my soul.
It encompasses my whole body as the still water
    from which my soul draws drink.
Its voice a whisper as a summer breeze,
    speaking peace, peace to my soul.
It must be the very voice of God that speaks
    light, love, and calmness to my soul.

FAITH

Faith is like a fire burning.
The more we feed it,
The more brightly it burns.

It is warm and glowing,
　　　all consuming.
Feed it not or all too lately
　　　it flickers and goes out.

The food of faith is our testimony.
The warmth is the Holy Spirit.
The glow is our love, our Christlike behavior.

Each one is intertwined, interdependent.
Take away one, you take away of three.
Oh, faith, burn brightly, burn warmly
　　　for I need thee.

PEACE BE STILL

How wonderful the words the Master spoke:
    "Peace, Peace be still."
It taketh the rage of the angry sea.
The tempest subsided, the winds calm, His will,
    "Peace, peace be still."

To those who will hear, the Master does speak:
    "Peace, peace be still."
Rage of our anger, so full and complete,
Emotions are bridled, no rage to defeat.
    "Peace, peace be still."

ENDURE

Before I came here
To the Lord I said
I will endure all, love all.
To Thee I shall return.

Now as that thin veil separates,
I sometimes forget my vow.
I think I cannot endure.
The pain grows so intense.

That tiny voice shouts out to me
In a great resounding voice,
"I will endure all, love all
To Thee I will return."

Answered from unuttered prayer,
My Father gives to me
The love, the peace, the strength I need
To endure all, love all, return, and live with Thee.

SERVE

To serve is to know joy,
The joy of helping, of loving,
Loving as our Savior did.
He served, He served us all.

His service, the ultimate of serving.
His love, the purest love of all.
Come taste of the goodness, the purity.
Serve, let joy swell in thy heart.

Love Is

Love is
A priceless gift
Passed on from one to another.
It is for giving,
Not taking.
It is like a flower,
Slowly unfolding its petals.
Love surpasses all time.
It is the essence of life,
Love is.

ACT 2

The second act is winding down; the final scene is playing.
Soon the intermission before unending act 3.
The second act we wrote ourselves, the scenes as we directed.
Act 3 depends on act 2; we cannot write another.
Has our act been strong enough, has it followed His example?
While time allows act 2 can change,
Act 3 depends on the revisions.

WHEN ONE QUESTIONS

At times I think myself weak,
Unable to bear, to endure to the end.
Why? Why am I here now
During the chaotic time before a new earth?

"You are here, my special child,
Because of your strength.
This you have earned,
To be on earth now,
To prepare for His coming.
You are among my strongest,
The best of the spirits, reserved.
I would never have sent you here now
If you could not return to Me.
Remember who you are.
Endure, endure well, and
Return unto Me.
I await thee."

At times when I think myself weak,
Unable to bear,
I remember who I am.
I remember His words
    He awaits.

THE GRAND LADY

The grand lady of the light,
She who avoids appearing as night,
One whose duty is to serve
From her righteous stand, to never swerve.

She who calls on the heavenly One,
Always striving to become
One at peace with the heavenly Son,
Following all His teachings, not just some.

This grand lady of the light
Walks in beauty, light so bright.
This grand lady exemplifies
All virtues so pleasing of the heavenly One.

YOU ARE SPECIAL

Sometimes we meet a special saint,
One for whom we see a spirit sweet.
Who uplifts all who chance to meet
    A special, special saint.

To you whose love is specially felt,
For you our love is freely given.
In faith go on the Lord's great mission,
    O special, special saint.

And as His agent thou shalt be
Enduring trials to set men free.
Remember: to Him you'll always be
    A special, special saint.

MY FATHER'S HOUSE

And now, in deep silence,
    with humble, contrite heart,
I enter into another place,
    far removed from this world.
Those hallowed walls sing of His love;
    peace, contentment encompass all.
It is in my Father's house that I feel
    most at home,
        most like His child.

THOUGHTS

And God said ... and it was
    a thought, a precious thought
    which sprang forth so righteously,
    was built and manifested
    and became the earth we see
    and became you and me.

And we think, and is it so?
    Our thoughts, a tiny thought
    that springs from deep within,
    are brought forth and manifested
    in the actions that we take
    and become our very life,
    the life that God does see,
    which shall judge you and me.

Our thoughts, most precious thoughts
    that we harbor deep within,
    some day will burst forth
    and become our life in deed.
    Take care in what is thought
    for some day it too shall be.

MY PRAYER

Dear Lord, help me to learn thy gospel.
    Show me the way that I should go.
Let me always be most humble,
    Teachable that I might grow.

Help me to understand that always
    There is something more to learn.
Guide me on the path of righteousness
    As Thy confidence I earn.

May I learn the joys in service,
    A comfort man may find in me.
Teach me, Lord, Thy precious lessons,
    So I each day may grow like Thee.

Teaching: No Greater Call

Before I passed through that thin and airy veil,
I conversed with the Lord about my new call.
"Of all the commandments I've given thee,
Remember, my child: always feed my sheep
And remember to teach; there can be no greater call."

As I passed through that veil shouting,
     "My turn to go,"
My conversation with the Lord started slowly to fade.
I turned and could not see Him; then a voice came
to me:
     "There is no calling greater heaven can give
     Than to teach one another to
          Feed My sheep."

ON BEING BLACK

Sometimes I cry out to the Lord,
    Why me, O Lord, why me?

If man is not charged with Adam's transgression,
Then why must the world look upon us as Cain.
Did not he commit the sin, not me?

"You are strong, you are special.
Your trials shall make you grow.
It is but a moment you suffer, you know.

I chose to make you black.
This trial you have won.
Be still, you are special, you are strong."

Sometimes I hear the Lord whisper to me,
    "Why not you, O special child, why *not* you?

JESUS THE CHRIST

Send down from heaven a holy gift
    To never more from Him to drift.
A special child of peace and praise,
    So we with Him to spend our days.

To live on earth just as a man,
    Life and power at His command.
Hallelujah, praise His name!
    Celestial glory He does reign.

His love He showed; praise to the Christ.
    Laid down His life in sacrifice.
Prince of Peace, Emmanuel,
    So we again with God may dwell.

THE HOLY GHOST

There is a small voice deep within,
Whose tiny voice is as one unseen.
This voice so strong, so confident,
Guides us in times both bright and not.

Who is this voice, from whence it came?
How does it know to keep us from pain?
It is a special heavenly gift,
The Holy Ghost, this is His name.

This gift is ours to keep or not.
To use we can, but not abuse.
Our friend can only grow in light.
In darkness He must take His flight.

This gift to you is given now
Remember only light to feed.
Keep Him always in your heart
For He will stay if you but do your part.

ADVERSITY

In life we have our many trials,
A test of faith how strong.
The good Lord knows what we can stand,
What trials to us belong.

He is so wise, so confident.
In each test growth we'll show.
I thank the Lord for adversities
So more like Him I'll grow.

GREAT AND TERRIBLE DAYS

Remember the times of struggle and doubt we read
Before the birth and death of Jesus they said,
"Prepare ye for that great and terrible day.
For the Lord cometh here to show the way."

We now live in that same kind of day.
Before the Savior in glory comes to show the way,
Prepare ye for that great and terrible day.
Prepare now, of this I fervently pray.

You Are Beautiful

Beauty most certainly is in the eye of the beholder.
And who beholds our hearts, our minds
And declares us a creation so beautiful?
None other than our Father, dear, whose
Wisdom is without question.

SERVICE

How blessed art thou, my faithful sister,
Serving the Lord in righteousness.
Helping another, showing the way,
Doing as He has asked.

Your dedication unsurpassed
In doing all that was asked.
He set the example for all to see
The happiness service can be.

SLOW OF TONGUE

I'm sorry that my words, my thoughts don't flow
easily.
I struggle to express myself in fluency,
Not knowing how I depend on the Spirit to impart
My thoughts, my cares, my words that are in my
heart.

Please listen, my friend, to the promptings within
your heart.
Those precious thoughts that come as I struggle to
talk
And know those thoughts, which the Spirit does
impart,
Are the words so sweetly said that I had sought.

THAT TINY SIN

It's such a tiny sin, I'm sure the Lord won't mind.
I've good reason, you see.
Just this once, this one time.
There, it's done, not at all too bad.

But then the empty feeling, and the tears begin to flow.
Oh, why did I, just this one time?
The rationale no longer holds.
The sin seems not so small.

On bended knee I plead and cry,
Forgiveness, please.
No sin is tiny, no rationale exempts; all sin is a crime.
Mercy tempers justice; oh, the price I had to pay.

I CRY

I cry, sometimes of sheer happiness,
sometimes from pure frustration.
Happiness because of the love Christ has for me,
frustration because like Him I think I'll never be.
Happiness because the Spirit has touched my soul,
frustration because I fail to reach another.
Happiness because someday I know I'll return to Him,
frustration because somedays I fail to strive.
Happiness because of the joys of service,
frustration at not giving my all.
I cry, but when I do, He's there to surround me
    as only a Father could.

DEATH

Death is but an open door,
Like unto the door through which we came at birth.
At birth we left the presence of our Father dear;
At death we again to His presence draw near.
Death is but an open door,
    nevermore to close again.

TODAY'S PRECIOUS WOMAN

Far more precious than diamonds or gold,
    Ever striving, ever becoming,
One whose spirit to the world has told,
    I am today's precious woman.

She has stored up treasures,
    Each a gem in her crown.
Rubies symbolic of love shown;
    Diamonds, symbolic of light learned;
Emeralds, symbolic of her great faith.

A crown upon her head she wears.
    A countenance of light, she glows.
A beauty sculptured by the hand of God,
    You are, my sister, today's precious woman.

FIND THE BLESSING

There is beauty in all things,
  all situations.
Sometimes it takes a little thought
  To see the blessings in it.
Find the beauty, take the blessings,
  Move closer in His love.

LISTEN

Learn to listen.
Listen ever so intently
To that small voice,
That tiny, tiny whisper.

That whisper so soft, so fleeting
Is the power, the source
That takes us home again
To Father, Mother, sisters, and brothers.

Learn to listen.
Listen ever so intently
To the voice, the source of all that's good.
Shh, shh; it speaks again.

COME UNTO ME

Come, little children, come unto me.
Hear the Word of your Lord.

Be seated there on holy ground.
Come listen to my Word.

Come drink of my fountain, eat of my fruit.
Rejoice in the Word of the Lord.

Come, my children, eat of the feast
The Lord for you doth send.

PAIN—JOY

Oh, the pain we cause our Father, Mother
     as we stroll through mortality,
Reaching out, touching, tasting
     the pieces of life's experiences.

Forgive us, Father, of the choices we make
     that causes Thou pain.

Oh, the joy our Father, Mother must feel
     when one such soul returns to the fold.
It is then we realize our Father's hand
     had always been there,
Reaching, straining to touch our souls.

Father, thank you for such love.
May we grow in thy sight, one day to behold.

SPECIAL TRUTHS

I. To him who is given much,
    Much is expected,
    And many are the trials.

II. The greatest trials give forth the greatest
    understandings and richest blessings.

III. Poetry is an expression of the spirit crying out.

IV. As faith without works is dead, so is desire without action.

V. A talent is not a talent unless it's shared,
    unless it reaches out to another.

Most Precious Gift

A child, most precious of God's sacred gifts,
Is given to you to raise in love and respect.
To teach him of the gospel is command'd
For him to follow the example Christ did set.

This child, a spirit child of God above,
In you does God put forth His trust
To one day return to his Father above,
Full of love, truth, knowledge, and respect.

TAKE MY HAND

Take my hand, thou beautiful sister.
Teach me the lesson thou knoweth I need.
Give me comfort, the strength I must muster.
Help me, my sister, to sow and to seed.

Take my hand, thou beautiful sister.
Let me teach thee the things of the Lord.
I will give thee comfort, dear sister.
Take my hand; together we seed.

STRENGTH IN UNITY

When there is strength in unity,
There is oneness in the heart.
When unity abounds,
Dissension has no part.

When there is strength in unity,
There is a song in every heart.
Happiness is seen throughout.
Love's spirit has been impart.

When there is strength in unity—
One mind, one heart, one thought—
Sacrifice for the greater good,
The spirit has been caught.

THE LIVING ANGEL

And God made man a little lower than the angels.
To some He gave a dual role:

"As you grow in mortality, my child,
You are to be a living angel.
Go forth to those who call my name.
Bring comfort and counsel to those in need.
They will feel your spirit and know.
Be strong, my child, for you have much to do,
       much to bear.
For thou art my living, loving, angel."

My Testimony

There is a testimony deep within that struggles to come out.
It must step over the blocks of fear and insecurity.
Oh, the testimony is strong; it lights the eyes and gives a
  countenance that glows.
It speaks in the actions of daily living, in service so freely given.

The testimony verbalized, one may rarely hear.
But to know of the testimony, one needs but to see
The little acts of love unasked, the joy of serving thee,
  sacrifice, and obedience all so willingly.
That Christ does live; the church is true.
  I try to show in all I do.

Today's Pioneers

No wagon trains upon unchartered paths,
No campfires under threatening skies,
No shallow grave or menacing mobs,
No physical hardships for today's pioneers.

Isolation, a few hard stares,
A longing to be part, to somehow fit,
Eager for a smile, a warm embrace—
Such mental hardships for today's pioneers.

Tears are many, come too often.
Hands reach out, encircling and embracing.
No more longing, no more tears.
Faith is rewarded for today's pioneer.

COMMUNICATION

You speak, but am I listening?
I listen, but do I hear?

I speak, but do I communicate?
You listen, but do you hear?

Wouldn't life be so much easier
If we spoke and communicated, listened and heard?

TEENAGER: HALF CHILD, HALF GROWN

O the tumultuous turmoil to all is known.
Along this path we all are thrown.
A raging storm within an open sea,
For a teenager, this is to be,
Half child and half grown.

O adult, oh, where is he?
And the child, is he now to be seen?
How are we to know which way to lean?
Confused confusion it is to be
Half child and half grown.

So take me tightly by the hand,
A port in a storm, that piece of land.
Help me to know, expand, and grow.
To learn of myself, my role I must know,
Half child and half grown.

COME

Come unto me, my precious child.
It is I, your Lord, who speaks.
Come take my hand; I'll lead the way
    To eternal life ye lead.

Come unto me, my precious child.
Through trials and lessons learn
The strength that they will give to you,
    So eternal life ye may have.

Come unto me, my precious child.
The way to me is love.
Do all I ask, do all I say,
    And share in all I have.

Spiritual Levels

There are times when I feel my spiritual level go

down,

down,

down.

I find many excuses—all others' fault—
To explain why this could be.

After listening to my list of woes,
Thou gently and firmly said to me,

"It was you who moved away from me,
Who walked the path of the world.
I called your name; you heard me not.
You wandered and did your will.
'Come back,' I called, 'lest you wander too far
And cannot find your way.'
I touched your heart in a special way,
And you heard me speak to you."

I heard His voice and turned around.
I ran to where He stood.

And now I feel my spiritual level
Going up by not small degrees.

THE PHONE CALL

I needed help; I needed to talk.
So I called up my wisest friend,
My closest kin, my spiritual adviser.

I talked and talked and talked some more.
Talking a long time, I asked many questions.
I exposed multiple emotions, from simple to sublime.

Having expended myself and stopping to catch
    my breath, I paused.
Starting to hang up, I heard Him call my name.
    He said, "I listened to you, now it's your turn.
    You called to ask my advice, to find answers.
    Why would you hang up before I could answer?
    Indeed, why call?"

"Why call," asked I, "isn't that what prayer's about?"
Gently but firmly He explained to me that
Each phone had a part for listening and talking,
Both to be used by each party.
If I had failed to listen, I had rudely hung up.
He would never, ever hang up first.

Joy in the Morning

When I give thought and reflect on the day,
My mind reels, and my heart gives way.
For battles fought and the turmoil of the fray,
Comfort comes; there's joy in the morning.

When I have done all there is for me to do,
And time no more governs what I strew,
Time for preparing I can no longer do.
Comfort comes; there's joy in the morning.

I WONDER

Sometimes I wonder—
With tears falling down—
If I'll ever make it
To my Father on high.

I wonder if perfection
Is obtainable for me,
Whether my works here and now
Are enough to pull me through.

Sometimes I wonder—
With tears rolling down—
If I've grown enough
To receive a small crown.

"Wonder less, my child.
Do all that thou can.
Read and see, hear and do
To behold the Son of Man."

A Purpose

A few minutes ago, in the sight of the Lord,
He sent you here to earth.
He sent you with a plan to fulfill;
With a purpose you did come.
You were sent for a season
Upon this earth, with purpose divinely given.
Have you done all you should?
Have you started His plan?
Are you ready to give Him report?
Of the things you have done,
Of your mission complete,
Will he say,
>   "Well done, my will not thine"?
>   Or will He look with tear in eye
>   And send another, His will to be done?
The season is now; do His will, choose the plan.
See a smile, not a tear in His eye.

If I have caused one heart to wonder,

If I have caused one soul to stir,

If I have caused new determination,

    Then I, in the cause of the Lord, resound.

Printed in the United States
by Baker & Taylor Publisher Services